Venus

Earth

Asteroid Belt

Saturn

Neptune

A Look at
Mercury

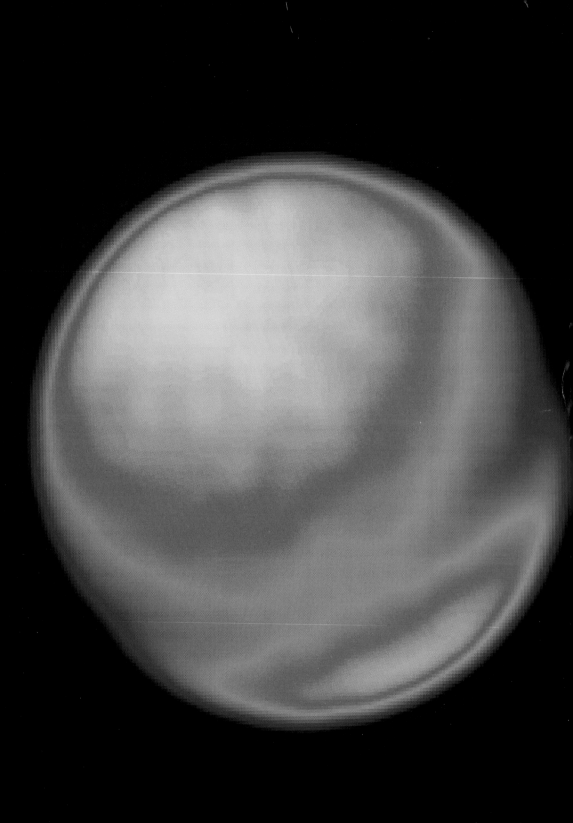

A Look at Mercury

Ray Spangenburg and Kit Moser

Franklin Watts

A DIVISION OF SCHOLASTIC INC.
NEW YORK · TORONTO · LONDON · AUCKLAND
SYDNEY · MEXICO CITY · NEW DELHI · HONG KONG
DANBURY, CONNECTICUT

The photograph on the cover is a photographic mosaic of Mercury compiled from
Mariner 10 images. The photograph opposite the title page shows a colored array
image of Mercury from the ULA telescope in Socorro,
New Mexico.

Library of Congress Cataloging-in-Publication Data
    Spangenburg, Ray, 1939–
    A look at Mercury / by Ray Spangenburg and Kit Moser.
    p. cm.—(Out of this world)
Summary: Describes the discovery and observation of the planet nearest the sun, Mercury,
including the findings of the Mariner 10 fly-by mission of 1974–75.
Includes bibliographical references and index.
    ISBN 0-531-11928-9 (lib. bdg.)   0-531-16673-2 (pbk.)
    1. Mercury (Planet)—Juvenile literature. [1. Mercury (Planet).] I. Moser, Diane,
1944- II. Title. III. Out of this world (Franklin Watts, Inc.)
QB611.S62 2003
                        523.41   dc21   2002008508

1 2 3 4 5 6 7 8 9 10 R 12 11 10 09 08 07 06 05 04 03

Acknowledgments

To all those who have contributed to *A Look at Mercury*, we would like to take this opportunity to say "thank you," with special appreciation to our editor, Melissa Palestro. We would also like to thank Melissa Stewart, who originally suggested this series and guided its early volumes. Additionally, we would like to thank Sam Storch, Lecturer at the American Museum of Natural History's Hayden Planetarium, and geologist Margaret W. Carruthers, who both reviewed the manuscript and made many insightful suggestions. If any inaccuracies remain, the fault is ours, not theirs. Finally, many thanks to Tony Reichhardt and John Rhea, our editors at the former *Space World Magazine*, who first started us out on these fascinating journeys into the regions of space, space science, and technology.

Contents

A Look at
Mercury

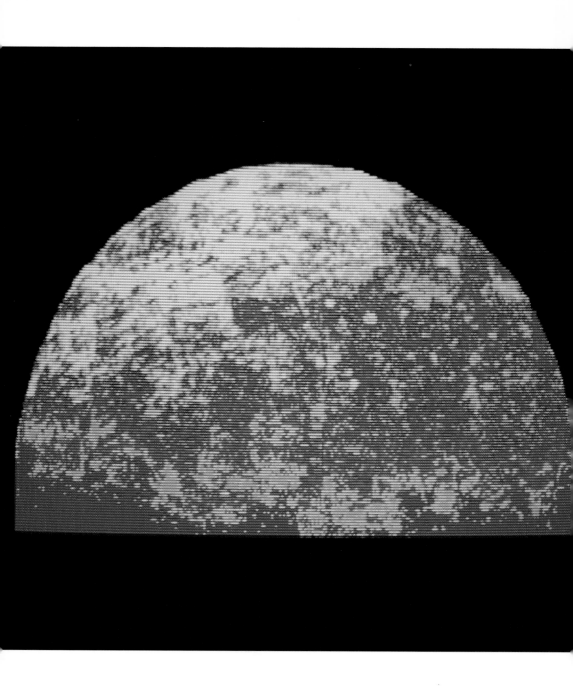

As this false-color photograph from *Mariner 10* shows, the surface of Mercury is heavily cratered.

Tiny Planet, Sun Skimmer

Blasted by the Sun's blistering heat, Mercury *orbits* closer to the solar system's star than any other planet. At its closest approach to the Sun, Mercury's distance from the Sun is only one-third that of Earth's. Temperatures on the side facing the Sun are searingly hot. On the other side, turned away from the Sun, temperatures drop in the frigid cold of space. Mercury has greater extremes of temperature than any other planet. This planet is a Sun skimmer, traveling in regions crossed only by comets, wayward *asteroids,* and the *solar wind*—a stream of highly magnetic particles that flows at high speeds from the Sun's surface.

After Pluto, Mercury is the smallest planet in the solar system. Mercury has almost no *atmosphere,* and its pockmarked, gray surface looks nothing like the green and brown continents and blue oceans of Earth, the cloud-covered surface of Venus, or the reddish mountains of Mars. It is nothing like the huge, gassy orbs known as the "gas giants"—Jupiter, Saturn, Uranus, and Neptune. In fact, Mercury looks a lot like Earth's Moon, and its *diameter* is only about 40 percent larger. Mercury has a diameter of 3,032 miles (4,879 km), while the Moon's diameter measures 2,160 miles (3,4765 km).

Mercury orbits so close to the Sun that for millennia astronomers have struggled to observe and study this elusive planet. The brilliant light of the Sun made Mercury hard to see. Only with new technology in the last fifty years have scientists begun to unravel some of Mercury's oldest mysteries. This book explores Mercury as we know it so far— but much exploring remains to be done. It is the only one of the rocky, Earth-like planets that has not been thoroughly mapped. So, scientists are planning a robot spacecraft mission to do just that. In future years, more information will be streaming in from Mercury, and scientists of tomorrow will be able to unlock many of the unsolved mysteries that remain. Perhaps you will have the opportunity to be one of those scientists!

Chapter 1

Mercury the Messenger

The nighttime skies are wonderfully entertaining and fascinating. They are filled with the lights of stars, galaxies, planets, and the Moon. Ancient observers watched these lights closely. They had little other entertainment after sunset. They couldn't watch TV or talk to their friends on the phone or read because there was no electricity. The nighttime skies captured their interest, and they gave deep thought to explaining the movements and arrangements of light they saw there.

To early humans, the stars, the planets, and other objects of the cosmos must have seemed a majestic and awesome display, as they appeared to roll across the skies overhead. One of the earliest known civilizations was Sumeria, which grew up from about 3000 to 1800

In Roman mythology, Mercury was the god of business and travel. Sometimes also called the messenger god, he wore a winged cap and winged sandals.

B.C.E. in the fertile regions between the Tigris and Euphrates Rivers in what is now northern Saudi Arabia and Kuwait. The Sumerians developed a form of writing called *cuneiform,* a system of drawings made with a sharp-edged tool on clay tablets. They Sumerians developed methods for keeping records, planned their crops, and created calendars to count the days of the seasons and nature's cycles. They left behind the earliest known astronomical records. Among those records were accounts of observations of what we call the planet Mercury.

The Sumerians noticed Mercury as a bright light that hovered near the horizon. It was not visible every night and could be best seen just before sunrise and just after sunset. The Sumerian name for this light was "Ubu-idim-gud-ud."

The Babylonians—another ancient people who recorded seeing Mercury—rose to prominence in the region now called Iraq beginning in about 1900–1800 B.C.E. Their name for the tiny light they sometimes saw at dusk and dawn was "gu-ad" or "gu-utu." The Babylonians were careful observers, and they made extensive records of the nighttime objects they saw. They were the first to trace Mercury's odd cycles, which are unlike the apparent movements of the other planets.

Egyptian and Chinese astronomers also noticed this tiny planet. The Chinese called it "Shui xing." The Egyptians thought of it as associated with one of their gods, Thoth, who represented the creative force in the universe.

The name by which we know this planet today comes from the Roman god Mercury, the messenger of the gods. He was patterned after the Greek god Hermes and was known for his speed; pictures of the god Mercury show wings on his heels and hat. The Roman and Greek gods were complex and had many associations. Mercury was the god of commerce (merchants), magic, and metals. In fact, Mercury gave his name to the metal mercury, also known as quicksilver, because the silvery metal is liquid at room temperature and moves fast, as if it were alive (an ancient meaning for "quick"). He also was gifted with language (as a messenger should be) and cunning, the god of travel and theft. The Romans probably saw a likeness between the speed of the messenger of the gods and the tiny, quick-moving planet that zipped so quickly across the skies.

The Roman system of gods and goddesses rubbed off on other civilizations that flourished in Europe to the north of Rome. So, "dies mercurii" ("Mercury's day") became Woden's day in the Nordic regions, or Wednesday on our calendars today. The Nordic god Woden was also a messenger of the gods and shared many of Mercury's traits.

Early Ideas About the Solar System

In ancient mythologies, the majesty of the skies seemed related to the realm of the gods. Most cultures thought of the planets as symbols of their gods or extensions of them. At the same time, as early as the Sumerians and the Babylonians, people gathered information based on observations of the planet they lived on and of the objects overhead in the skies. These observations became important as they worked out their calendars, planned their crops, and learned about nature's cycles. These kinds of activities were the earliest beginnings of science—the process of putting together a body of knowledge built on observations and experiments. From this information, scientists develop *hypotheses* and theories about the universe around us.

Ancient observers noticed that a group of objects seemed to wander across the skies at a different pace from the rest. The word "planets" comes from the Greek word meaning "wanderers," used by Greek astronomers to describe this difference. In addition to Mercury, the ancients observed the planets we now know as Venus, Mars, Jupiter, and Saturn.

In some early theories about the universe and how it works, Earth was seen as the central pivot for everything. The Sun, the stars, and all the planets supposedly revolved around Earth. This idea seemed logical, given the way all these objects seem to rise, cross the sky, and set. So the *geocentric*—or Earth-centered—view of the universe was favored in many ancient cultures.

As early as 356 B.C.E., though, a Greek astronomer named Heraclides (c. 390–310 B.C.E.) put forth a different idea. He suggested that if the heavens held still and Earth *rotated* on an *axis,* the effect would look the same for people watching the skies from Earth's surface. Heraclides also noticed that both Mercury and Venus always seemed to remain very close to the Sun. This seemed suspicious to him. Why would this be true? He suggested that maybe—just maybe—Mercury and Venus did not revolve around Earth. Maybe they revolved around the Sun. This point of view is often called *heliocentric,* or Sun-centered. He was the first person to suggest that Earth might not be at the center of everything. However, his idea was not very popular in his time, and many centuries went by before it had much influence.

Most early Greek philosophers continued to embrace the geocentric theory, and the great Greek philosopher Aristotle (384–322 B.C.E.) gave his stamp of approval to it. However, over time, astronomers kept making careful observations and recording their data. They noticed that some of the planets did not behave the way they should if they revolved around Earth. One astronomer, Ptolemy of Alexandria (100–70 B.C.E.), suggested some elaborate "fixes" for the theory in the second century A.D. His explanations were very complicated, but they satisfied astronomers for several more centuries, until 1543. In that year, a Polish astronomer named Nicolaus Copernicus (1473–1543) published a book, *On the Revolutions of the Heavenly Spheres.* To support his conclusions, Copernicus had used careful mathematical calculations based on observation. He suggested that Earth rotates on

The great Greek philosophers Aristotle (right) and Plato (left) both taught Heraclides, who was the first to suggest that Mercury orbited the sun. Both Aristotle and Plato, however, believed that the planets orbited Earth.

an axis and revolves around a stationary Sun, and he showed how much more sense this heliocentric view of the solar system made.

Old ideas sometimes die hard, though, and Copernicus's ideas came under fierce opposition. However, in 1609, a litte more than fifty years after Copernicus's death, the telescope was invented. The Italian astronomer and physicist Galileo Galilei began using a telescope to examine the planets and stars. He sketched the phases of Venus—sometimes a slender crescent, sometimes a full disk, sometimes somewhere in between. He also noticed that when Venus appeared as a full disk, it looked much smaller than when it appeared as a crescent. Astronomers had noticed that Mercury also went through similar phases. What caused these changes of light patterns from a planet? If these two planets orbited the Sun inside an orbit traveled by Earth, then an observer on Earth would sometimes see the Sun's light reflected on the full disk of either inner planet. Or the sky watcher might see more than half, but not all, of the disk reflected in the Sun's light. That would happen only if Mercury or Venus was traveling on the other side of the Sun from Earth, and so the planet would be much farther away. When its lit surface appeared as just a skinny crescent, it was traveling closer to Earth, between Earth and the Sun. So, it appeared larger. These observations were consistent with the idea that the planets were traveling around the Sun—not around Earth.

Galileo campaigned courageously for Copernicus's ideas, even though he was directed not to do so by authorities of the Catholic Church. By the middle of the seventeenth century, people began to understand that Earth rotates. They saw that this *rotation* causes the heavens to appear to move around Earth. They also began to see that Earth moves around the Sun—the Sun does not move around Earth.

The Polish astronomer Nicolaus Copernicus is generally credited with proposing that Earth and the other planets were part of a solar system, in which they revolved around the Sun.

By this time, too, the invention of the telescope had changed the way people thought about the other planets. Now they could see the round disk of these spheres against the nighttime sky. The planets were no longer just pinpoints of light, aimless "wanderers" among the stars. People began to realize that these objects were other "worlds," possibly a lot like our own.

Since that time, many scientists have tried to find out more about these other worlds. Are there other ways in which the other planets and Earth are similar? What can the structure and history of other planets tell us about our own? How did all these objects around us get here? How did Earth get here? Where did the planets come from? Why are there four "terrestrial," or rocky, Earth-like planets, close to the Sun?

Beginnings

No one saw the universe begin. Yet—based on calculations and observations of the universe today—astronomers have a pretty good idea how it must have happened. They think that at the beginning of time, everything began with an event known as the Big Bang. "Everything" means everything in the universe—everything we can see or touch or detect, everything that can in any way affect us. Astronomers think this colossal explosion of something incredibly tiny and hot took place about fifteen billion years ago. Everything that exists today came initially from the hydrogen and helium that formed at the time of the Big Bang. From that moment, the universe began expanding, and it has been getting bigger ever since.

Some people wonder if there could be other universes, or whether another universe existed before the Big Bang. No one really knows. Scientists have only been able only to discover evidence of this universe and its history.

Birth of a Star

About 4.6 billion years ago, in the galaxy we call the Milky Way, a cloud of gas and dust began to gather together. It was one of many such clouds in the Milky Way. Over time, the cloud, or *nebula,* grew bigger and bigger. Swirling constantly, it grew huge, trillions of miles across. As more time passed, the rotating cloud center began to shrink inward upon itself. As the *mass* in the central region

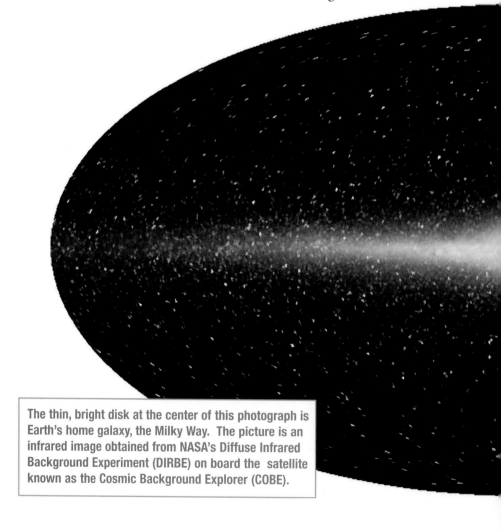

The thin, bright disk at the center of this photograph is Earth's home galaxy, the Milky Way. The picture is an infrared image obtained from NASA's Diffuse Infrared Background Experiment (DIRBE) on board the satellite known as the Cosmic Background Explorer (COBE).

became greater, this material began to contract even more. The material at the center kept getting denser, and its gravitational pull kept getting stronger. So more and more material was attracted and pulled in, and the material at the center continued to collapse in upon itself.

More *interstellar* gas and dust (from between the stars) fell into the center of the nebula, and the temperature and pressure rose. At the dense center, hydrogen atoms began to break up into their

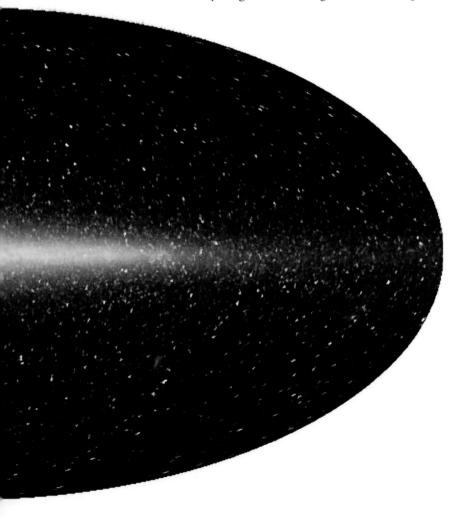

sub-atomic particles—*protons* and *electrons*. Protons (particles with a positive charge) repel other protons. But now the collapsing cloud's strong *gravity* and extreme motion overcame that repelling force. *Nuclear fusion* began to take place, joining protons together. Several steps later, hydrogen atoms (with one proton in the *nucleus*) turned into helium atoms (with two protons and two neutral particles called neutrons). The process released an enormous amount of energy. The result was even greater heat and an even greater release of energy. What was once a huge cloud of dust and gas had become a colossal hydrogen bomb! At that moment, a star was born—just as many others had been born and were beginning throughout the galaxy and all the galaxies of the universe.

This particular star was our Sun. Of course, no one was there to see our Sun form, any more than anyone was present when the universe began. However, as long ago as 1755, a German physicist and philosopher named Immanuel Kant first came up with the idea that stars form from a disk of gas and dust. No telescopes were powerful enough, though, to look at stars that were just forming. So, no one had seen a disk of gas and dust of the kind Kant was describing, but the model made sense. Scientists worked on Kant's initial idea for many years—creating models, later analyzing *meteorites,* and looking for other clues. One problem was: how could anyone see the forming star at the center of a dark mass of swirling gases and dust? When astronomers began to train *infrared* telescopes on suspect areas, though—telescopes that could "see" temperature differences—they found that they could finally peer through the clouds. When they did, they began to find disks of gas and dust with infant stars beginning to

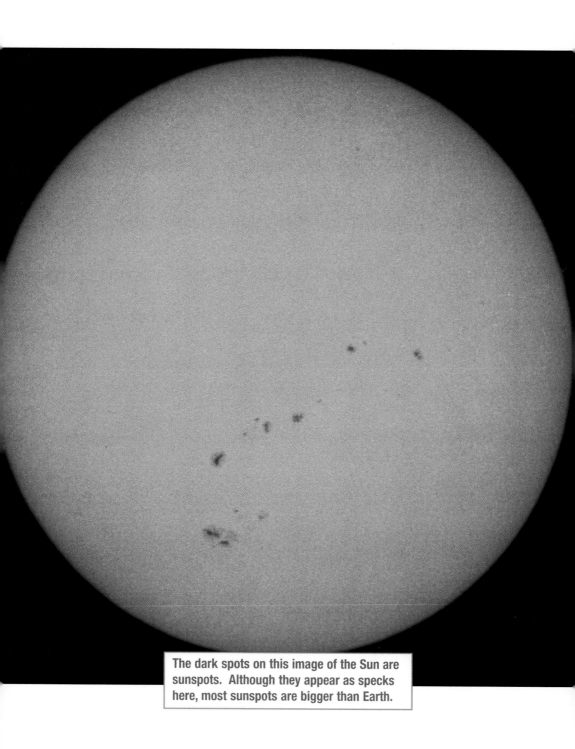

The dark spots on this image of the Sun are sunspots. Although they appear as specks here, most sunspots are bigger than Earth.

Although best remembered today as a philosopher, Immanuel Kant also did important scientific work, particularly regarding the creation of stars.

form at their centers. More than two hundred years after Kant's work, in the 1980s, astronomers began to find conclusive evidence of stars forming within disks of gas and dust.

Rocks Around the Sun

Surrounding the infant star we call the Sun, the huge disk of hot gases and debris continued to swirl, and gradually the disk began to cool and condense, forming solid masses. Most astronomers believe that the first solids were very small. Then these joined together to form bigger pieces. Those joined together to form even bigger chunks. Clumps of matter the size of houses or bigger began to form. The bigger they became, the more gravitational attraction they had. They became attracted to each other and formed even larger bodies that were the size of asteroids. This process is called *accretion*. Before long, runaway accretion began to take place as big objects began smashing into each one another. Eventually, larger and smaller masses formed, including what later became the planets and moons of our solar system.

Some debris was not swept up into the planets and moons, though, including large chunks of rock and ice that number in the trillions. These make up the asteroids and comets that also orbit the Sun, scattered throughout the solar system. Other, smaller chunks called *meteoroids* also form part of this system today. These are almost all bits that have broken off various moons, asteroids, and planets sometime since the formation of the solar system. A wide band of asteroids orbits in a region known as the a*steroid belt,* located between Mars and Jupiter. Others cross orbits with Mars and Earth. Still others even masquerade as moons—such as Phobos and Deimos, the two moons of Mars. As we recently discovered, even asteroids (sometimes known as "minor planets") can have moons. Comets—composed of ice and rock surrounded by a cloud-like halo—travel around the Sun in long orbits that originate on the remote outer edge of the solar system. When a comet travels close to the star's warmth, coming or going, a tail of vaporized ice appears. The tail always points away from the Sun, pushed by the solar wind.

Sometimes one of all these chunks ran into another and shattered into billions of pieces. Or small chunks collided with larger ones—planets or moons—and combined with them. These violent, wild collisions have slowed since the early days just after the Sun was born, but they have not stopped. The solar system is still a place where objects crash into each other. Such collisions produce trillions of smaller pieces of rock called meteoroids.

The Hard-to-See Planet

Mercury stands out among all these solar system objects and all the planets as one of the least explored. Some people even call it the "forgotten planet." Since ancient times, astronomers have faced big challenges when they tried to observe Mercury. The planet is tiny, and it always travels close to the Sun. So the glare and brightness of the Sun make seeing this tiny orange dot of a planet much more difficult. It also puts in an appearance far less frequently than the other planets, peeking above the horizon in early morning or early evening only a few times a year. When you observe an object in the sky so close to the horizon, you are peering through the thickest part of Earth's atmosphere. The wavery distortion produced by this thick air makes Mercury's small, reddish disk seem to heave and wobble. Observers have few opportunities for watching Mercury, and when they do the view is usually brief, fuzzy, and wavy.

So as thousands of years went by, astronomers learned more and more about the other planets, but Mercury remained a mystery in many ways. Until quite recently, no one had any idea how long a day on Mercury was

So far, scientists have seen only one side of
Mercury. Is its other side as heavily cratered?

Science—Not Just Being Right

The Italian astronomer Giovanni Virginio Schiaparelli (1835–1910) was well respected in his time for his attention to detail and his dedicated observations of objects in the solar system. He graduated from Turin University in Italy in 1854, and after graduation he studied for six years with eminent astronomers in Germany and Russia. In 1860, he returned to Italy to become director of the Brera Observatory in Milan. He held that position until his retirement in 1900.

During his career, Schiaparelli made many contributions to solar system science. He was the first to recognize that meteor showers—sometimes known as "falling stars"—are caused when pieces of debris left behind by a comet plummet into Earth's atmosphere and burn up. He is also known for his discovery of the asteroid Hesperia in 1861.

In spite of his solid reputation, though, Schiaparelli is best known for his mistakes. While carefully observing Mars in 1877, he observed lines he called *canali*, or "channels." He saw what appeared to be straight lines forming a network among the *canali*. Most other astronomers could not see the structures Schiaparelli detected, and perhaps he should have taken more note of this lack of an important principle of science: the ability to duplicate the results of an experiment or confirm an observation. Schiaparelli, though, felt sure he had found confirmation during later observations.

Some astronomers, however, took these observations far beyond Schiaparelli's dry descriptions. They interpreted *canali* to mean "canals"—structures built by intelligent beings to transport water. The idea caused a media blitz and caught the public's imagination, creating a furor that went far beyond Schiaparelli's intentions. For decades, many people continued to think that an irrigation system or other artificially constructed network of canals might exist on Mars—built by intelligent extraterrestrial beings. Not until spacecraft finally visited Mars and took close-up images in the early 1970s did people recognize that the connecting lines Schiaparelli thought he saw were caused by an optical illusion.

Schiaparelli also observed some streaks across the surface of Mercury a

(period of rotation) was or how long the little planet took to travel around the Sun (period of *revolution*)—two of the most basic facts.

The first astronomer to detect any features on Mercury was a German astronomer named Johann Hieronymous Schroeter (1745–1816). He sketched what he saw in detail, including a mountain, which he few years later, in the 1880s. However, these did not look straight, and so no one imagined they might be canals. While watching these streaks over several years, Schiaparelli observed that the streaks always appeared in the same relative place on the planet's disk. He concluded in 1889 that one side of Mercury always faced the Sun—and that only one side of the planet could be observed from Earth. So, he said, Mercury's "year" (a full revolution around the Sun) was the same length as its "day" (a full rotation on its axis). Later, as you will see, astronomers found that Schiaparelli was wrong about this, too.

However, science is not just about being right. (In fact, in many cases, it isn't possible to determine for sure if you definitely *are* right.) Instead, science is more about finding the best interpretation of all the available objective evidence. At any given time, science attempts to provide the clearest insights based on what is observed. However, science corrects itself. When new evidence comes to light, scientists may have to rework their interpretations and theories. Schiaparelli

It took Giovanni Schiaparelli eight years to make his map of Mercury.

observed carefully and collected data. He was a good scientist, and other scientists have gone on to use his experience to build their understanding of the objects he observed.

estimated to be 12 miles (19 km) high. The master of English astronomy, William Herschel (1738–1822), looked for Schroeter's mountain and other features he had sketched, but he couldn't see them. Even the best observers of the time found peering through telescopes too difficult for finding surface features on Mercury. They could not overcome the disadvantages of observing this small planet that was always positioned within a few degrees of the Sun.

By the late 1800s, Mercury had captured the curiosity of the great Italian astronomer Giovanni Schiaparelli (1835–1910). He saw smudged streaks across the surface, somewhat similar to structures he had seen on Mars. However, no one else was able to see what he saw.

In the early 1930s, another astronomer tried his hand at drawing a map of the features on Mercury's surface. Greek astronomer Eugenios Antoniadi (1870-–1944) used the 33-inch (84-centimeter) *refracting telescope* at the Meudon Observatory in France. It was small by today's standards, but it was a good telescope. A few years earlier, he had done an exquisite job of drawing maps of Mars using the same telescope. His Martian maps were so accurate that, years later, when robot spacecraft visited Mars and sent back pictures, every feature he had drawn showed up on the images—proving the high quality of his work.

Antoniadi's maps of Mercury serve as testimony to his many patient hours of observation and careful draftsmanship. He recognized that the distortion caused by Earth's atmosphere would make his job nearly impossible if he attempted to map Mercury as it hovered close to the horizon. So, he observed Mercury in broad daylight, when it—and, of course, the Sun—soared high above the horizon. Looking at an object so close to the Sun is very risky to one's eyesight. (Note: never look directly at the Sun—you can do severe damage to your eyes, even possibly cause blindness.) Also, the features he saw were flooded with light—showing very little contrast of light and shadow. Even so, he observed Mercury as often as he could, and he published his map in 1934. It showed many details—including mountains, plains, and swirling dust. Antoniadi gave these areas romantic names, such as

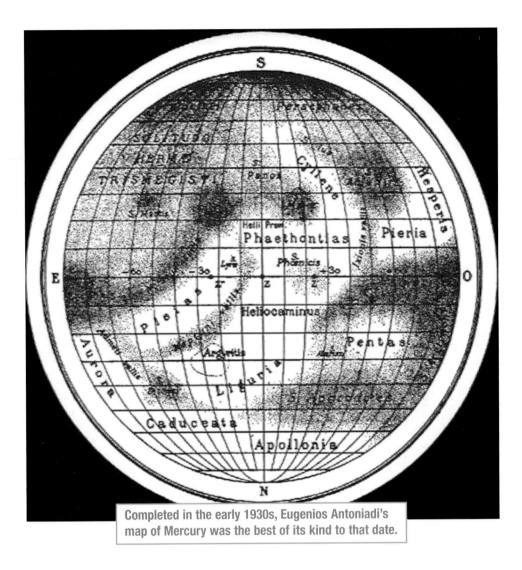

Completed in the early 1930s, Eugenios Antoniadi's map of Mercury was the best of its kind to that date.

Aphrodites (recalling the Greek goddess of love) and Apollonia (after Apollo, the Sun god). Antoniadi's map was the best view of Mercury that anyone had ever captured. But was it good enough?

Even as recently as the 1930s, Mercury, the "messenger of the gods," was not carrying very clear messages to Earth's astronomers.

This photograph, taken by *Mariner 10*, shows an area of about 90 by 105 miles (144 by 170 kilometers) on the surface of Mercury. The crater just left of the center of the photograph measures about 7.5 miles (12 km) across.

Chapter 2

At Last, Closer Views

No one could blame early astronomers for their problems with Mercury. With the instruments they had, Mercury posed an impossible problem. Finally, though, the early 1960s to the 1970s brought some exciting breakthroughs. At last astronomers could begin exploring the "forgotten planet."

Explaining an Anomaly

Anomalies are important in science. An anomaly is a fact that doesn't fit the rest of the pattern—a piece of information that doesn't follow the rule or is not what you might expect. In science, growth comes from noticing anomalies and trying to explain them. If something doesn't fit, maybe the hypothesis needs to be adjusted. Maybe a new way of thinking is required. Maybe just a little tweaking needs to be done. Or maybe the facts have not been gathered accurately. In any case, when facts and interpretation are out of step, when an anomaly exists, change will probably be required sooner or later.

An anomaly about Mercury had bothered astronomers for a long time. It had to do with Mercury's orbit. Isaac Newton's laws of gravity, laid out in the late seventeenth century, predicted that astronomical bodies would would influence each other's orbits. For example, Newton's laws of gravity predicted that the gravitational mass of Venus, Earth, and even Jupiter would cause Mercury's orbit to be a highly *eccentric orbit*—much longer than it is wide. So, astronomers were not surprised when they measured Mercury's orbit and found that it ranged from 44 million miles (70.1 million km) at its farthest point to within 29 million miles (46.7 million km) of the Sun. (In fact, Mercury has the most eccentric orbit of all the planets except Pluto.) However, Mercury's point of closest approach to the Sun (*perihelion*) is moving—advancing around its orbit. Or to describe it another way, the entire ellipse is rotating so that both the long axis and the short axis shift, slowly marching in step around the Sun over many decades. This effect is known as *precession*. Newton's laws do not explain why Mercury's orbit kept keeps changing in this way—at least, not as much as it does! So Mercury's orbital precession was an anomaly.

Astronomers suggested possible explanations. Maybe a mass of fine dust between the Sun and Mercury would exert enough influence to cause the point of closest approach to move. However, no such cloud of dust was ever detected. But something had to be causing the precession astronomers saw.

In the mid-nineteenth century, the French astronomer Urbain Leverrier (1811–1877) predicted the existence of a planet beyond Uranus in the outer solar system. (At about the same time, the English astronomer John Couch Adams made the same prediction.) In 1846, based on Leverrier's calculations, German astronomer Johann Gottfried

Having predicted the existence of Neptune, Urbain Leverrier wrongly surmised that anomalies in Mercury's orbit could only be accounted for by the existence of another planet between it and the Sun.

Galle found the planet Neptune—right where Leverrier and Adams said it would be.

So, when Leverrier looked at the problem with Mercury's orbit, he thought along the same lines as when he discovered Neptune. At first he suggested that a second, smaller asteroid belt might be located between Mercury and the Sun. Then in 1859, he received a letter from an amateur astronomer, who reported seeing a round, black spot on the Sun. He thought it might be a planet. Leverrier fell in love with the idea, and he even named the planet Vulcan. Many astronomers searched for years for Vulcan and for signs of smaller asteroids that might explain the oddities of Mercury's orbit, but no one ever found anything.

Finally, when the American physicist Albert Einstein published his *General Theory of Relativity* in 1915, he laid the groundwork for explaining the anomaly of Mercury's movements. According to Einstein's theory, the enormous mass of the Sun "bends" all nearby space-time so much that its effect on Mercury's orbit would be easily observable. German astronomer Karl Schwarzchild provided the calculations in 1916—and the figures worked out exactly. The calculations explained the anomaly and also provided a validation of Einstein's theory!

As for Leverrier's planet Vulcan, photographs taken during a solar eclipse in 1929 showed no sign of it. With the Sun's light dimmed by the eclipse, any unknown object the size of Vulcan should have shown up. Later, in about 1970–1971, some researchers thought they saw Vulcan during a solar eclipse (when the Moon blocks out the Sun as seen from Earth). However, they probably just saw a comet passing close to the Sun.

Taking a "Look" with Radar

At about the time Antoniadi was mapping Mercury in the 1930s, a new astronomy technique known as radio astronomy was born. This branch of astronomy began in 1931, when Karl Jansky (1905–1950) of Bell Telephone Laboratories in New Jersey first discovered radio waves coming from space. Scientists now know that all objects in the universe actually give off radio waves. These radio waves can be gathered and measured by *radio telescopes* that look like huge satellite dishes. The first studies of radio signals from the universe began in 1937.

By 1958, an ingenious concept for a giant radio telescope was born. William E. Gordon, a professor of electrical engineering at Cornell University in Ithaca, New York, came up with the idea of making use of an enormous limestone *sinkhole* near Arecibo, Puerto Rico. This natural, bowl-shaped valley measures 1,000 feet (3,005 meters) across and acts like a gigantic satellite dish. Its huge size enables it to collect very faint and distant signals from the far reaches of the universe. Today, it still has the largest collecting area of any single radio telescope in existence. A platform, suspended high over the huge bowl of the telescope, carries equipment to send and receive radio signals. Researchers can point this equipment at different parts of the sky to examine specific objects.

Meanwhile, astronomers had also begun using *radar* to examine far-off objects in space. The word "radar" stands for *ra*dio *d*etection *a*nd *r*anging, and it is just another way of using radio signals. During World War II, the military used radar to locate enemy aircraft by pinging (bouncing) radar signals off an aircraft's exterior. Astronomers found they could use the same method to find out more about nearby objects

Nestled in a natural valley, the Arecibo radio telescope measures nearly 1,000 feet (300 m) in diameter and consists of almost 39,000 surface panels.

in the solar system. For example, using radar, scientists could bounce signals off the surface of Mercury and detect the planet's features. Then they could use these observations to time the rotation. That is, the period of rotation is equal to the elapsed time between the first detec-

tion of a unique feature on the surface of the planet and the next detection of the same feature.

By 1962, the Arecibo radio telescope (which is able to transmit as well as receive radio signals) had established radar contact with Mercury. After that, it was just a matter of time before astronomers began to use this new technique to find out more about Earth's second closest neighbor.

By 1965, G. H. Pettengill and R.B. Dyce were able to use radar observations from Arecibo and made a breakthrough. They finally figured out how long Mercury took to complete one rotation. One day on Mercury, they discovered, equals more than 58.6 Earth days!

So Schiaparelli had been wrong. Mercury's day is not 88 Earth days long—it is much shorter. However, his mistake was understandable. With an orbital period of 88 Earth days and a rotation period of 58.6 days, Mercury completes its tour around the Sun in about three Earth months and takes about two Earth months to make one rotation on its axis. This ratio of three to two means that every other year on Mercury, the same side faces the Sun. If Schiaparelli had been right— if the orbital and rotational periods had been exactly the same length of time—the same side of Mercury would always face the Sun. But this was impossible to realize in Schiaparelli's time.

Ice at the Poles?

The three-to-two ratio between Mercury's rotational and orbital periods produces some strange temperature conditions on its Sun-baked surface. Both day and night last for months at a time, and two areas on the surface receive intense, repeated exposure to the Sun's fierce heat. Located on opposite sides of the surface, these areas are sometimes known as "hot poles." When the planet makes its closest approaches to the Sun, the temperature is scorching hot—as high as 800° Fahrenheit (4257° Celsius)—making Mercury one of the hottest places in the solar system. Practically no atmosphere exists on Mercury, so the heat just radiates directly back out into space instead of spreading

Tools of Science: Radar Astronomy

Astronomers can bounce powerful radio signals off the surface of a nearby planet, moon, or asteroid—Mercury, for example—to find out more about its rotation, orbit, and surface.

Using the technology known as radar, the radio transmission must be set at a precise frequency. It is usually controlled by an atomic clock and it uses closely spaced, exactly timed pulses. Many precise adjustments must be made continually to allow for Earth's rotation and movement around the Sun. The signal travels to the target object, bounces, and returns to Earth. When the signal arrives, the radio telescope captures it and feeds it to the receiver and the analytical equipment. The equipment measures, very precisely, the time the bounced signal took to make the round-trip.

The returning signal usually echoes from several different areas of the object being measured, with different frequencies depending on the area, so analysts can recognize the position of a particular feature. By repeating the pings at different times, they can measure the movement of the object. That's how Pettingill and Dyce figured out the true length of Mercury's day.

Today, radar *resolution* has become more and more refined. In 2002, scientists announced the capture of radar reflections off a prominent crater 53 miles (85 km) wide. A splash of bright rays some 560 miles (900 km) across may mean that the crater is surprisingly young. The resolution in this study is ten times greater than any previous radar study of the area—showing radar to be a continuing resource for unlocking Mercury's secrets.

to other regions of the surface. (On Earth, the atmosphere absorbs a lot of the heat.) Meanwhile, on the side facing away from the Sun, temperatures plunge to extreme subfreezing temperatures of about –279° degrees F (–173° degrees C). So, Mercury is also one of the solar system's coldest locations.

Even the average temperature on Mercury's surface is extremely hot: 354° degrees F (179° degrees C). So *planetologists* were stunned by a discovery made in 1991 by a team of scientists from the California Institute of Technology. They were bouncing radio waves off Mercury to find out more about the planet's terrain. When they looked at the results, they found some small, strangely bright areas of unusual radar reflections near the poles. These "radar bright" reflections are not necessarily optically bright, but they are typical of radar reflections caused by patches of ice. They suggest that ice deposits may lurk near the poles of Mercury, away from the concentration of sunlight. Researchers believe that comet collisions may have sprayed frozen material into the shade of big rocks or deep craters and crevices in these areas. Or possibly water vapor in Mercury's thin atmosphere has frozen into frost caps. The long shadows cast by the Sun in these regions may preserve a permanent deep freeze—allowing ice to form right at the Sun's back door!

Viewing the Sun from Mercury

Remember that Mercury makes two trips around the Sun for every three times it rotates (the "three-to-two ratio"). In addition, Mercury's orbit is very eccentric—that is, the orbit is an ellipse, not a circle, and it is much longer than it is wide. Also, when Mercury is traveling close to the Sun, it travels much faster than when it is far away. At certain points in Mercury's trip around the Sun, these facts combine to produce some strange consequences—"strange days," as some people like to call them. Imagine that you are an astronaut standing on the surface of Mercury. (Of course, probably no one will ever do this!) As you ride the planet during its closest sweep by the Sun, you watch the sunrise one morning, only to see everything you know about sunrises completely fall apart. It is possible that you would see the Sun rise twice above the horizon in one Mercury day!

Comparing Mercury and Earth

Vital Statistics

	Mercury	Earth
AVERAGE DISTANCE FROM THE SUN	0.39 AU* (36 million miles; [58 million km])	1 AU* (93 million miles; [150 million km])
ONE ORBIT AROUND THE SUN	87.9 Earth days	365 Earth days (1 year)
DIAMETER AT EQUATOR	3,032 miles (4,878 km)	7,927 miles (12,755 km)
SURFACE GRAVITY	0.38	1
ATMOSPHERIC PRESSURE AT SURFACE	Almost zero	1 bar
COMPOSITION OF PLANET	Nickel-iron, silicates	Nickel-iron, silicates
MASS	0.055	1
VOLUME	0.056	1
DENSITY	5.43 grams/cm³	5.52 grams/cm³
TILT OF AXIS	0 degrees	23.5 degrees
COMPOSITION OF ATMOSPHERE	Hydrogen, helium (trace amounts)	Nitrogen, oxygen, argon, carbon dioxide, water

* 1 *AU (astronomical unit) (AU)* is the distance between Earth and the Sun

Its proximity to the Sun has contributed to the difficulties in studying Mercury.

Why? For a moment, just about four days before closest approach, the planet's speed of rotation is precisely the same as its orbiting speed. Because of this, the Sun travels east to west across the black, airless skies. But then it seems to stop when the two speeds exactly match—and then appears to reverse directions, traveling west to east. That's because Mercury rotates faster than it travels around the Sun during the time of its closest approach. The Sun continues to cross the skies from west to east for about four days. Then things go back to normal. But getting there would not look normal. The Sun would rise in the west about halfway, then set, and finally rise again.

Going There to Take a Look

Astronomers are known for their uncanny ability to find out a lot about places that are enormous distances away. However, there's nothing like visiting in person, and the next best thing is to send someone to take pictures and measurements for you and send back information from an on-site visit. The study of Mercury received a big boost in 1974 and 1975 when an unmanned, or robotic, spacecraft paid Mercury just such a visit. Finally, planetary scientists—and all the rest of the world—had a chance to take a much closer look at Mercury.

The visitor was *Mariner 10*, launched by the U.S. National Aeronautics and Space Administration (NASA) in 1973. It was a small spacecraft, about the size of a horse, powered by two solar panels that could easily fit in most closets. *Mariner 10* was the seventh successful launch of the *Mariner* series of spacecraft, and it was heavily insulated against the Sun's torturing heat to protect its sensitive equipment. Onboard, in its instrument compartments, it carried numerous tools for measuring the atmospheric and surface characteristics it would observe during its voyage. These tools included a television camera, a magnetic field experiment, instruments to measure infrared and *ultraviolet* radiation, and radio science detectors. This little spacecraft is so far the only visitor ever to make the voyage to the tiny innermost planet.

Originally, Mariner 10 was a mission to Venus, with no plans at all for visiting Mercury. However, as they planned the trajectory, or flight plan, for the spacecraft, NASA scientists realized that a few small adjustments would allow a very unusual flight path past Mercury. *Mariner 10* was the first to use what NASA calls a "gravity assist." As *Mariner 10* neared Venus, it made use of Venus's gravitational pull to give it a boost. The boost swung the little spacecraft on its way to Mercury. Space scientists have used this trick many times since the 1970s to make the most of a spacecraft's journeys.

Most *flyby* missions—such as the Voyager missions—are one-shot glimpses of the planets, moons, asteroids, or comets they pass. Then they whiz on to the next site on their itineraries, finally zooming off,

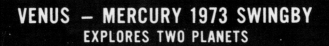

VENUS – MERCURY 1973 SWINGBY
EXPLORES TWO PLANETS

VENUS

INTERNAL MASS DISTRIBUTION; THERMAL REGIME; ATMOSPHERE & CLOUD CHARACTERISTICS

MERCURY

PRESENCE & STATE OF A CORE; MAGNETIC FIELD; SURFACE CHARACTERISTICS; THERMAL REGIME; ATMOSPHERIC DETECTION

NASA SL69-1083
6-30-69

This illustration by a NASA artist outlines the plan for the *Mariner 10* Venus-Mercury swingby mission of 1974-75 and what NASA hoped to study about each planet.

sometimes even leaving the solar system, in an endless voyage through space. Eventually, they lose contact with Earth completely. However, the *Mariner 10* planners realized they could arrange an enormous bonus for their mission. Because of Mercury's unusual orbital patterns,

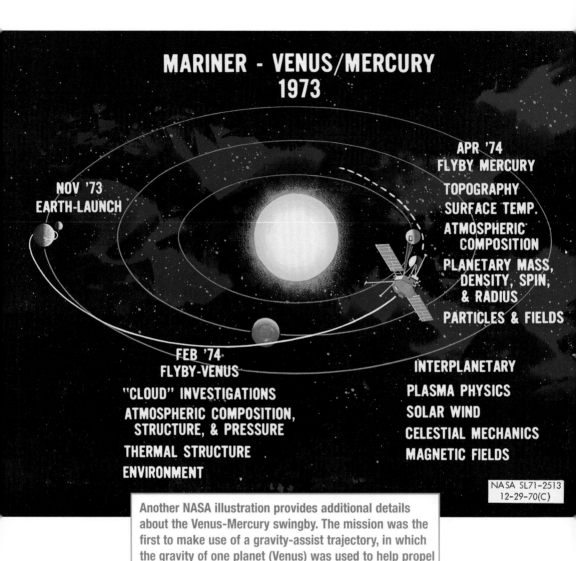

MARINER - VENUS/MERCURY
1973

NOV '73
EARTH-LAUNCH

APR '74
FLYBY MERCURY

TOPOGRAPHY
SURFACE TEMP.
ATMOSPHERIC
COMPOSITION
PLANETARY MASS,
DENSITY, SPIN,
& RADIUS
PARTICLES & FIELDS

FEB '74
FLYBY-VENUS

"CLOUD" INVESTIGATIONS
ATMOSPHERIC COMPOSITION,
STRUCTURE, & PRESSURE
THERMAL STRUCTURE
ENVIRONMENT

INTERPLANETARY
PLASMA PHYSICS
SOLAR WIND
CELESTIAL MECHANICS
MAGNETIC FIELDS

NASA SL71-2513
12-29-70(C)

Another NASA illustration provides additional details about the Venus-Mercury swingby. The mission was the first to make use of a gravity-assist trajectory, in which the gravity of one planet (Venus) was used to help propel the spacecraft on its way toward the second (Mercury).

Mariner 10 was able to make one trip around the Sun and encounter Mercury three times! This was the chance to take the first close-up looks ever at the planet nearest the Sun.

Science at Work: Getting a Boost

In the early days of exploring the planets, NASA engineers came up with an idea for going farther on less fuel and packing more missions into one spaceflight. When a spacecraft is launched, every ounce of fuel adds to the weight that the launch rocket has to lift into space. For every drop of fuel added to the cargo, more fuel has to be added to propel the launch rocket. So, mission planners and engineers thought of another plan: Why not use the gravitational pull of other planets as the spacecraft goes by? This plan has the added advantage of allowing the spacecraft to do additional science and testing on the way.

The *Mariner 10* mission was the first time NASA scientists ever tried this trick, called a "gravity boost." On its way to Mercury, the spacecraft skimmed by Venus first, on its way to Mercury. On the way past Venus, it took pictures and collected data about Venus. Then it arced around the planet and zoomed off toward Mercury.

Since then, NASA has used this trick over and over on spaceflights to study the Sun, the outer planets, and the edges of the solar system.

When *Mariner 10* finally arrived at Mercury, scientists quickly discovered that they were in for a lot of surprises. For its first pass, on March 29, 1974, the spacecraft was scheduled to whiz by for a quick look, very close to the planet, only 438 miles (705 km) from the surface. There, *Mariner 10* made three surprising observations. First, Mercury has a magnetic field. (Earth is the only other rocky planet with a magnetic field.) Second, Mercury has an atmosphere—not much of an atmosphere, to be sure. But before the Mariner 10 mission, scientists didn't think it had any at all. Third, the *crust* of Mercury proved to be of very low *density*. From observations made from Earth, scientists already knew that, overall, Mercury was nearly as dense as Earth. So the lightweight crust was slightly unexpected, too.

For the first time, observers realized that Mercury is covered with wide, shallow basins that look a lot like the craters found on the Moon

This is the southwestern quadrant of Mercury, as photographed by *Mariner 10* on March 29, 1974, when the spacecraft was 122,000 miles (198,000 km) from the planet. The largest craters visible are about 100 miles (160 km) in diameter.

and Mars. The photos were clear enough to show craters as small as 100 miles (160 km) across. Unfortunately, the spacecraft's closest approach brushed past Mercury on the night side only—the side unlit by the Sun. Without light, *Mariner 10* couldn't take photographs. However, on the first pass alone, *Mariner 10* transmitted about two thousand photos of Mercury's lit side back to Earth.

The second pass took place on September 21. This time *Mariner 10* took a more distant look at Mercury, from 29,900 miles (48,01090 km)—a good distance for large-scale mapping. The spacecraft took photos of the sunlit side of the planet, including the region around the south pole, mapping 45 percent of the planet's surface.

Finally, on March 16, 1975, the spacecraft made its final pass, speeding by Mercury for one last look. This time it was traveling at a very low altitude, 200 miles (320 km). It took about three hundred final photos, but that was not its main mission on this run. Scientists wanted a closer reading on the planet's magnetic field, and they established that Mercury's magnetic field is not just part of the planet's environment. That is, it is not an effect of the solar wind. Instead it really is generated by the planet itself. This result was not what most scientists expected at all.

On March 25, 1975, *Mariner 10* ran out of fuel for controlling its attitude, or orientation, so the project scientists had to end the mission. The little spacecraft had done a great job, sending scientists on Earth almost three thousand images and much data to work from. Some thirty years later, the images and data are still providing new insights as scientists find new ways to learn from *Mariner 10*.

This illustration provides a cutout view of Mercury's interior. Most of its interior consists of a large, iron core.

Chapter 3

Puzzling Inside Story

Mercury, Venus, Earth, the Moon, and Mars are not just huge chunks of rock traveling around the Sun. They are made up of layers. The solid surface is the thin outermost layer, or crust. The layer beneath the crust, the mantle, is in most cases the largest layer of a planet. At the center is the *core*. It is made of heavier elements that sank to the center when the planet first formed and was still hot and mostly molten.

Mercury's interior is odd, though. Scientists are still puzzling over the story of Mercury's interior as reported by *Mariner 10*. Unlike the Moon, with its small core, the little planet has a giant core for its size. This core is probably made of iron, which could explain the enormous density of the planet. Scientists think this metal core makes up about

75 percent of Mercury's diameter and 42 percent of its volume—a huge proportion of the total planet! The size of Mercury's core is one of its great mysteries.

Mercury: Massive Yet Petite

The planet Mercury is incredibly massive for its size. Its diameter at the equator measures 3,032 miles (4,879 km), just slightly smaller than Jupiter's giant moon Ganymede, which measures 3,273 miles (5,2687 km) at the equator. Yet Mercury has twice Ganymede's mass!

Of all the planets in the solar system, only Earth is denser, and then only slightly denser. That is, compared to Earth, Mercury has nearly as much mass, or material, per unit of volume. *Mariner 10* scientists used the spacecraft's interaction with the planet to get a measurement of Mercury's gravity. They found out that even though Mercury's volume is three times greater than the Moon's, the little planet exerts a gravitational pull more than twice as strong as the Moon. At 5.43 g/centimeter, its density (a measure of how tightly it is packed) is almost as high as Earth's (5.52 grams per /cm). Mercury also seems to contains at least twice as much iron as any other planet in the solar system. Scientists estimate that its core must be very large, taking up to about 65 to 75 percent of the planet. As a result, some people call Mercury "the iron planet."

All the *terrestrial planets* (the rocky inner planets—Mercury, Venus, Earth, and Mars) are thought to have a dense core rich in iron. Generally, the crust of all these planets formed like a "skin" across the top of hot pudding. When materials in the mantle melted, lighter materials floated to the surface, and solidified. Denser materials settled to the center, forming a dense core. What's amazing about Mercury, though, is that its core is so large, so dense, and so rich in iron. Also, Mercury seems to show very little iron in its surface rock and dust.

Scientists have proposed three different ideas about why Mercury's core is so big. But so far no one has found sufficient evidence to be sure which one is right. One idea is perhaps when the planet formed, thin

The prevailing theory holds that our solar system was formed from the dust and debris of a solar nebula, shown here in an artist's conception.

What Is a Theory?

You probably hear the word "theory" often. Many people have a lot of vague ideas about what a theory is, though. Maybe it's easier to begin with what a theory is *not*. It is not a loosely worded, untested possibility. It is not just an idea.

In science, a theory begins first as a hypothesis. A hypothesis is a carefully thought-out statement that a scientist thinks is worth exploring further to find out whether it is true or not. However, it has to have another trait: it must be a statement that researchers could prove false—if it is false. It must be a statement that can be tested. For example, the statement "I like chocolate" cannot be tested. You just have to take the speaker's word for it (or not), but there is no way you could prove whether he or she really does like chocolate or not.

Once a hypothesis passes tests and experiments, it still doesn't become a theory overnight. It has to hold up under many experiments or observations, by many different scientists, many times. Only if the results continue to be consistently valid can the tested hypothesis be called a scientific theory.

Even then, the testing is not over. A good theory makes "predictions"— events or situations that researchers can look for. If the predictions are true, the theory gains more validity. If not, it may come under question. For example, as you'll recall, Karl Schwarzchild's calculations in 1916 showed that Einstein's *General Theory of Relativity* predicted the precession of Mercury's orbit. That fact helped validate Einstein's theory. By the time you see a discussion of a theory in your textbooks, it has probably survived many, many tests. For example, Einstein's general theory of relativity has survived hundreds of tests, and many predictions have verified it.

Even so, a theory is never completely "proven." If it were, it would become a fact or a law. New facts or observations can cause scientists to look at a theory in a new way. Science is "self-correcting." That is, scientists constantly search for better answers about the universe and how it works. A theory is a tested hypothesis that has not yet been proven wrong. At any given point, though, a theory represents one of the best ideas we have found so far—after careful, methodical testing.

gases from the *solar nebula* slowed heavier substances enough so that they tended to clump together more than lighter substances in Mercury's neighborhood. Thus, Mercury ended up with more dense metals, such as iron. At the surface, though, its makeup was much the same as all the other planets—mostly composed of rocks made of a material called silicate.

Another idea proposes that early in the planet's development, the nearby Sun's tremendous heat caused the outer layer of rock to evaporate. Only the planet's dense iron core was left behind. Meanwhile, heat given off by radioactive substances may have created a kind of furnace that remelted Mercury. In the resulting molten mass, dense metals, such as iron, would have sunk to the center to form Mercury's dense core. If so, this happened at least three to four billion years ago. Finally, when the planet cooled, all that was left was the heavy, scorched cinder of metal that we see today.

The third theory is that an ancient asteroid collision may have caused the small planet's very high proportions of metal. Computer simulations show that a glancing blow from a large asteroid could have blasted off most of Mercury's less dense surface rock and rocky mantle. Finally, all that was left behind was its iron core. This theory may explain why Mercury is nearly as dense as Earth. If Mercury once had more bulk, made of light materials, then its density may once have been much more like the Moon's. Did Mercury lose its light rocks in some early catastrophic impact?

More Questions

Not all the questions about Mercury's *composition* would be answered by these theories, though. How can you determine the composition, or makeup, of a planet? One method scientists use is called "spectroscopy"—the use of the *electromagnetic spectrum* to tell what things are made of. Each chemical element has its own spectroscopic "signature." Spectroscopy translates this information into a code that

Science at Work: Using Spectroscopy

The light we see is part of an important family of energies known as the electromagnetic spectrum (the full range of the waves and frequencies of electromagnetic radiation). Visible light is just about in the middle of the spectrum—the portion of the spectrum that we describe as the different colors of the rainbow, from red to violet. Red is made up of longer wavelengths of light, while violet is made up of shorter wavelengths. White light (sunlight and starlight) is a mixture of many of these colors. The rest of the electromagnetic spectrum is made up of types of radiation that humans cannot see, including radio waves and radar.

Everything has its own characteristic spectrum. That is, every object absorbs some wavelengths of light and reflects others. For example, grass (actually the chlorophyll in grass) reflects a lot of wavelengths in the green part of the spectrum. Goldfish reflect a lot in the yellow and orange parts of the spectrum. When we look at things and observe their color, we use a natural form of spectroscopy to identify them by their color. Spectroscopes can identify these wavelengths precisely, as well as the portions of the electromagnetic spectrum that humans can't see, such as infrared, ultraviolet, and radio waves. Scientists use spectroscopes to analyze, in detail, the full spectrum of light reflected from a particular material. It's sort of like a bar code. Then they compare that spectrum to the spectra (plural of "spectrum") of materials they already know about. This is how we know, without landing on Mercury, that there is very little iron in the surface layer of this little planet.

identifies which parts of the Sun's white-light spectrum are reflected from the surface of the planet. With this information, scientists can tell what the surface is made of.

Mercury's surface shows us very little iron in its surface rock and dust, leaving scientists puzzled. How could there be so little iron in the surface composition when Mercury apparently has a very large iron core? What process drained all the iron out of the surface and dumped it into the core? On Earth, considerable quantities of iron remain in the surface layers, even though our planet also has an iron core. What made Mercury different?

Old Volcanoes?

Most of Mercury's surface is covered with craters, but in some areas the terrain shows smooth, unblemished plains. What could have caused these smooth plains? What is this smooth material made of? Is it material from volcanoes, similar to the plains of the Moon known as maria? Or were they caused by *ejecta,* the material thrown upward and outward by large impacts?

Another *Mariner 10* image shows the craters on Mercury's surface. The material around the crater is known as the ejecta blanket. It consists of debris thrown up from the crater when it was being formed.

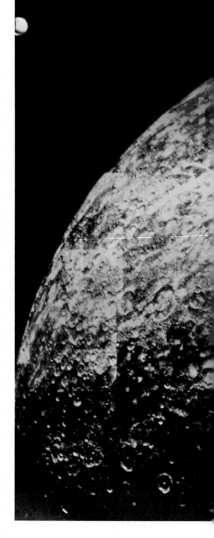

Sometimes it pays to look again at material in the planetary archives. That's what two researchers are doing with data from *Mariner 10* collected more than twenty-five years ago. Planetary scientists Mark Robinson and Paul Lucey have used recent improvements in computers and image-processing to take another look to see if they could find the answers to these questions. Then they compared pictures of Mercury taken from Earth with the ones taken at Venus and Mercury. The science team also studied samples of rock from the Moon in laboratories. They compared how the Moon reflects light. They began to make some breakthroughs in understanding how the way you look at reflected light affects what you see.

Robinson and Lucey knew that if the smooth plains on Mercury were volcanic, they should have a slightly different composition from the regions surrounding them. After all, lava comes from inside the planet and flows over the rocks on the surface, covering them up. Unless the lava is made from exactly the same material, lava plains should look different from the rest of the surface. Ejecta material is just pulverized surface material, so it should have exactly the same makeup as the rest of the surface.

The research team applied color codes to images taken by *Mariner 10*. They used one color to show the presence of dark-colored minerals

Its closeness to the Sun and irregular orbit leaves Mercury with the greatest temperature variation of any planet or natural satellite in our solar system.

and another to show the presence of iron. Then they matched the color-enhanced maps with other information they had gathered about the surface. From the combined facts, they could were able to make some good guesses about the history of Mercury's interior.

They found that the smooth plains do look different from the surroundings—on the color-coded map, the plains are slightly different in color from the cratered regions. The scientists believe that these plains regions are a lot like lava plains on the Moon, formed by volcanic activity—ancient volcanoes that erupted long ago on Mercury and laid down lava beds. Some of these volcanoes may even have

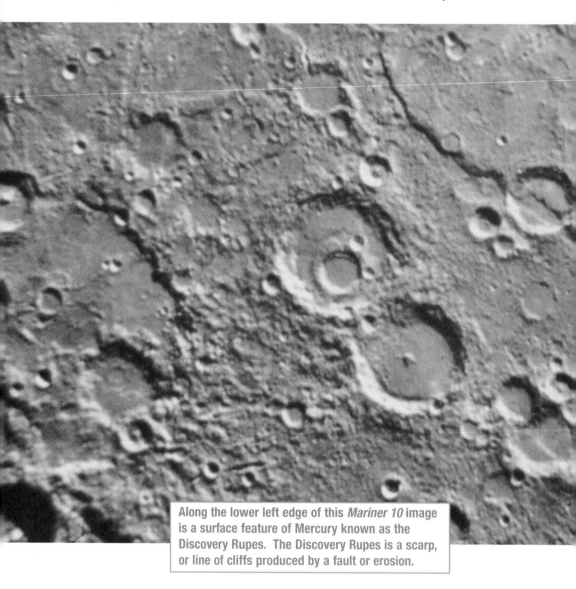

Along the lower left edge of this *Mariner 10* image is a surface feature of Mercury known as the Discovery Rupes. The Discovery Rupes is a scarp, or line of cliffs produced by a fault or erosion.

erupted after some of the worst collisions took place during the early formation of the solar system some three to four billion years ago.

By studying *Mariner 10*'s images in new ways, these researchers have begun to learn more about the planet's interior—what it is made of and what happened there. However, their work does not answer all the questions. Were the volcanic eruptions fluid, oozing out onto the surface? Or were they explosive? Are all the smooth plains volcanic?

Scientists need more information to be sure. Possibly some of the plains on the planet were not formed by volcanoes. Instead, they may have formed when heavy rains of rock fragments and dust peppered the surface after a huge impact.

Still Liquid Inside?

One of the big questions about Mercury's interior remains: Is it liquid? As you have seen, one of the big surprises reported by *Mariner 10*'s voyage to Mercury was the presence of a magnetic field. Magnetic fields, most scientists thought, were created when rotation caused currents in a core that could conduct electricity. Like a dynamo, they thought, the planet's rotation and the movement of liquid in the core created the magnetic field. Mercury rotates very slowly, though—only once every 58.6 days. Also, most scientists thought the core of Mercury was solid, not molten. So no one expected it to have a magnetic field.

However, *Mariner 10* discovered one on its first flyby and confirmed more about the magnetic field on its last pass. Scientists began to ask: Is this another anomaly? Maybe the current theories about planetary magnetism were wrong. Many Mercury planetologists want to send another mission to Mercury to find out more.

Mariner 10 images such as this one, taken from 19,300 miles (31,000 km) away on March 29, 1974, provided scientists with some of the first conclusive evidence that Mercury's surface had likely been shaped by a combination of tectonic and volcanic activity and collisions with foreign bodies.

Chapter 4

Craters, Rocks, and Gases

Before *Mariner 10*'s visit to Mercury, no one knew that this tiny planet's exterior was covered with craters. Mercury's battered surface shows thousands of scars where meteorites, asteroids, and comets have smashed into it for millennia. Most of Mercury has a rough, rugged terrain, dotted with craters, much like the Moon, Mars, and Jupiter's moon Callisto.

So, on the outside, like the Moon, Mercury is pockmarked by ancient craters and currently appears to have no internal activity at all. The *Mariner 10* images do not show signs of any recent volcanic activity or lava flows. The smooth lava plains amidst the battered terrain were probably formed long ago when molten material spilled out from

Formation of a Crater

When a smaller object crashes into a much larger one, it leaves a hole or depression in the surface, called an *impact crater*. For example, when a meteorite smashes into Mercury's surface, the impact's energy breaks up material on the surface, melts it, and *ejects* it (throws it upward and outward). Where the meteorite strikes the surface, a saucer-shaped indentation, or crater, forms. Below the saucer bottom, the rock is fractured.

Above, pieces of broken rock and rubble may shoot up and fall back to the surface. When they land, they often create smaller craters (called secondary craters) around the main crater. Also, if the hit is huge enough, it explodes and vaporizes. So the impact is not simple a simple dent, but an explosion crater. Many, many meteorites have bombarded Mercury's surface in the past 4.5 billion years, and the pockmarked face of the little planet tells the story.

the planet's interior. However, no one is really sure how these vast smooth areas formed, although perhaps the new evidence described in the last chapter gives some clues. In any case, somehow these few areas have avoided most of the hits.

A Cratered Tale

Scientists think that the many craters we see on the surfaces of Mercury and of Earth's Moon tell the story of a time long ago in the history of the solar system when many objects crossed each other's paths and collided. They sped across the space between planets and moons and smashed into anything in their paths. Scientists know from studying the Moon's craters and rocks brought back from the Moon that many more collisions occurred early in the solar system's history— and every object in the solar system, including Earth, has been hit many, many times. (We don't see as much evidence on Earth because processes such as erosion by wind, rain, and flowing water have wiped away the scars.) So in all likelihood, many objects smashed into the small planet during its early history. More recently, Mercury, like the rest of the solar system, has taken far fewer hits.

Mercury's surface and the Moon's surface look like they share a similar history—heavy bombardment followed by filling with molten lava. Both surfaces have also gone billions of years without significant change.

The Big Hit

When you look at one side of Mercury, you can't help noticing the biggest known feature on the surface of this small planet. It is called Caloris Basin, a huge, round, ringed depression with no outlet. (The name "Caloris" comes from the Latin word "calor," which means "heat." The word "calorie" is formed from the same word.) Caloris Basin is one of the two "hot poles" on Mercury's surface that face the Sun directly when the planet orbits closest to the solar furnace.

The Caloris Basin is 800 miles (1,300 km) across, and it looks a lot like the large, circle-shaped, multi-ringed basins found on the Moon. Scientists think an asteroid or comet smashed into Mercury early in its history to form Caloris Basin. Later, lava probably erupted inside the crater, filling it and smoothing it out.

Mariner 10 captured images of about half of this huge crater, the part that was lit by the Sun when the spacecraft passed overhead. The image shows the eastern edge, where huge rough blocks about 2,500 to 6,500 feet (760 to 2,000 km) high are thrown up along the rim. To the northeast, hills and mountains spread out from the rim like rays of light from the Sun. To the east, lumpy plains stretch out into one of Mercury's mysterious smooth plains.

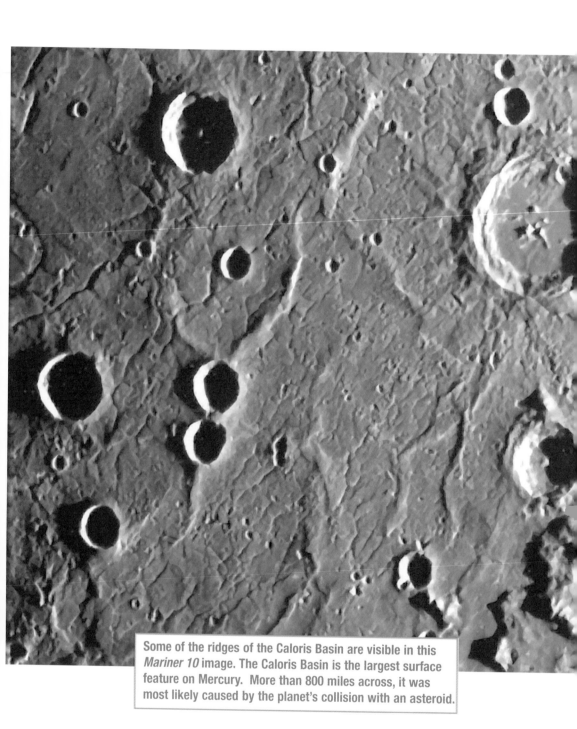

Some of the ridges of the Caloris Basin are visible in this *Mariner 10* image. The Caloris Basin is the largest surface feature on Mercury. More than 800 miles across, it was most likely caused by the planet's collision with an asteroid.

A series of ridges and fractures along the smooth basin floor have puzzled scientists. Some believe these ridges are caused by the crumpling of geologic layers or strata caused by sideways pressures. Others insist that volcanic lava flows have formed the ridges as molten material pushed up through fractures in the basin floor.

Most scientists agree, though, that a tremendous smash hit must have jolted the planet about 3.85 billion years ago. It was the second-largest recorded impact on any of the four rocky planets, caused by a huge, asteroid-like object about 95 miles (150 km) in diameter. When this huge collision took place, the energy released by the explosion was equivalent to a trillion 1-megaton hydrogen bombs. The giant impact caused shock waves that rumbled all the way around and through the planet.

Surface Jumble, Ridges, and Cliffs

On the other side of the planet, a region of rough rock and crust breaks up into a chaotic series of jumbled blocks. Geologists describe this hilly, rugged area as "weird terrain," covering a territory roughly as large as France and Germany together.

Researchers think the Caloris Basin impact may have sent shock waves heaving through the crust as surface waves. At the same time, compression waves may have passed through the planet's core. Within minutes, all these forces would have collided and focused on the opposite side of the planet. As a result, ragged hills and valleys cut across other hills and valleys. The ground would have shot upward as far as about half or two-thirds of a mile (805 m or 1 km). As a result, researchers believe, the planet's crust suffered the deep fractures that we see, and great blocks of material were dislodged. Nothing like this

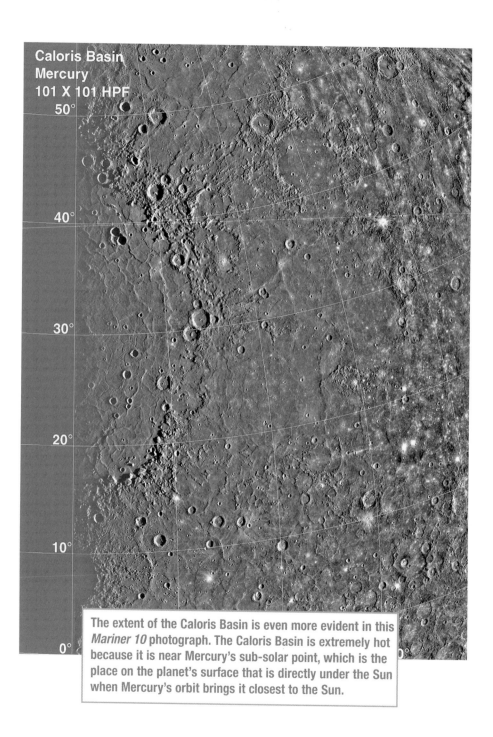

Caloris Basin
Mercury
101 X 101 HPF

50°

40°

30°

20°

10°

0°

The extent of the Caloris Basin is even more evident in this
Mariner 10 photograph. The Caloris Basin is extremely hot
because it is near Mercury's sub-solar point, which is the
place on the planet's surface that is directly under the Sun
when Mercury's orbit brings it closest to the Sun.

region of chaotic, contorted rubble has been seen anywhere else in the solar system, so it is difficult to know exactly what did cause it, but this is a "best guess."

Elsewhere on the little planet, *Mariner 10* discovered enormous cliffs, called "lobate scarps," that cut across surface craters. These cliffs are thought to have formed billions of years ago, as the young planet cooled and shrank. The planet contracted and its skin shriveled, causing *thrust faults*. As the compressive force on the crust built up, the rocks broke, and one huge block of crust would rise. Meanwhile, the block next to it sank. These cliffs cut across mountains, valleys, and craters. They extend for hundreds of miles—up to 300 miles (484 km) long. Some tower up to 13,000 feet (4 km) high, nearly as high as Hawaii's biggest mountain, Mauna Kea.

Mercury, the "Dead" Rock

Mercury's terrain is covered with dust, caused by billions of years of pummeling by the pieces left over from the formation of the solar system. Some of the colliding objects are very small—chips called "micrometeorites" that are tiny, microscopic pieces of asteroids, meteorites, and comets.

Another force, called thermal erosion, creates even more dust. Between daytime and nighttime, huge temperature swings of more than 750° F (400° C) cause the rocks to expand with the heat and contract with the cold. This continual expansion and shrinking of Mercury's skin causes pieces of rock to chip off and crumble to dust.

From the condition of the craters, planetary scientists can deduce the "age" of Mercury's surface. Most of Mercury's many craters are almost as deep and jagged as the day they formed, when a big rock came whizzing through space and smashed into the surface. Not much else has happened on Mercury to change the way these craters look. There are no rivers flowing through the craters to wash away the walls. No volcanoes erupt to fill the giant holes with lava and melted rock. No winds blow on Mercury to shift the dust and wear away the edges. The erosion caused by forces of weather, water, and volcanoes on Earth does not exist on Mercury. The only erosion on Mercury's surface is caused by the tiny impacts from thousands of micrometeorites, the expanding and shrinking of the surface skin, and gravity.

Scientists have figured out the age of the big craters on Mercury, and they can see that the craters have remained almost untouched by geological activity for billions of years. In geological terms, Mercury has been dead for about 3 to 4 billion years. That's why some scientists call it the "dead rock" close to the Sun.

The surface of Mercury tells scientists many stories. By studying images from *Mariner 10,* scientists have learned a lot about Mercury's history—even though they are the first to say that much remains to be learned.

Some scientists think that Mercury may once have been twice as large as it is today, cut down to its present size by a huge impact in the planet's distant past. That theory seems to fit with a few other facts about Mercury.

The huge Caloris Basin tells the story of at least one enormous jolt. If a giant collision did take place, that could also explain why Mercury has such an odd orbit. The little planet averages a distance of 36 million miles (58 million km) from the Sun. But that's just an average. As you have seen, Mercury actually swings very close, within

Color was added to this *Mariner 10* image of Mercury. Scientists believe the light blue areas may be ancient volcanoes.

As one of the four terrestrial planets, or "rocky planets," Mercury is part of the group that also includes Venus, Earth, and Mars. The surfaces of these rocky planets and their moons show evidence of many events that have taken place since they formed. As erupting volcanoes spread hot lava over a surface or meteorites crash into it, these events leave behind a visible history. At the same time, parts of the previous record are destroyed. Geologists use these clues on the surface to read a planet's history.

Mercury shows few, if any, signs of geological activity for the past three billion years or so. As a result, many ancient features are still intact. Geologists can read its surface like a book containing records of events that happened as far ago as three billion years ago. Like detectives, geologists can read all this history from the pictures and information that our robot spacecraft sent back to Earth.

28.6 million miles (46 million km). Then it swings much farther away in a long loop, to a distance of 43.3 million miles (69.7 million km). The orbit may have been flattened by a major collision early in Mercury's history.

All these pieces of the past seem to fit together. Finding out for sure, though, will require still more exploration!

Atmospheric Surprises

Before *Mariner 10*'s visit to Mercury, scientists had detected no atmosphere on Mercury. That was no surprise—presumably, the planet is so close to the Sun that gases would be cooked out of the interior by the Sun's searing heat and escape into space. So *Mariner 10*'s discovery of an atmosphere on Mercury was totally unexpected. It is very thin, to be sure, extraordinarily thin, only a billionth the density of Earth's atmosphere.

However, *Mariner 10*'s ultraviolet spectrometer confirmed the results of its testing beyond any doubt. It detected the presence of helium, hydrogen, and oxygen, with helium being the most abundant. Later, in 1985, Earth-based observation of scattered sunlight using spectroscopic analysis showed the presence of sodium atoms, too. The following year, the same technique also found small amounts of potassium in Mercury's atmosphere.

The atmosphere's atoms are constantly lost by the planet, but they are also constantly replaced. Charged particles from the solar wind are one source. Also, Mercury's *magnetosphere* serves to direct a few atoms toward the planet's surface. Meteoroid impacts also send particles flying upward from the surface. These hits from "space rocks" also bring particles in, though, and they probably provide the source for the potassium and sodium detected in the atmosphere. Small contributions may also come from a few other sources. Overall, while Mercury's atmosphere is not much to talk about, its discovery is another example of science's self-correcting process. No one thought there could be an atmosphere on Mercury. Scientists found out that wasn't true, and added this new piece of knowledge to the growing store of our understanding of the solar system and how it works.

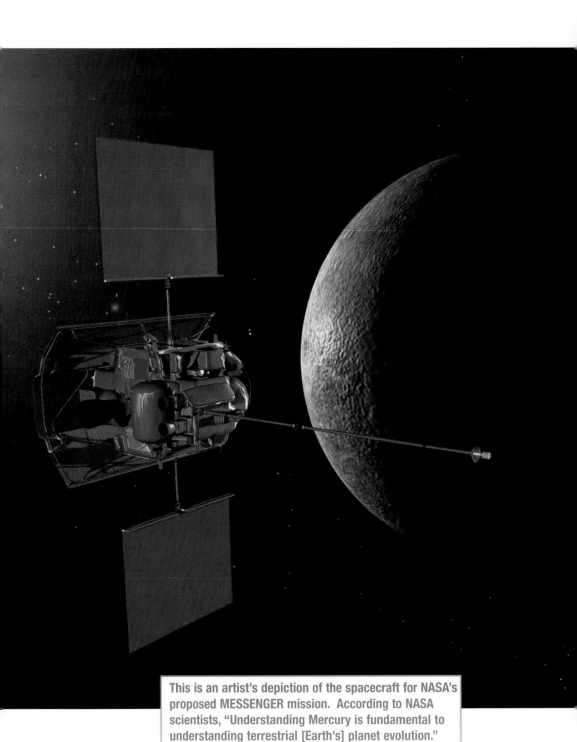

This is an artist's depiction of the spacecraft for NASA's proposed MESSENGER mission. According to NASA scientists, "Understanding Mercury is fundamental to understanding terrestrial [Earth's] planet evolution."

Chapter 5

Continuing Mysteries

ariner 10 gave scientists their first real look at Mercury. It suc-
ceeded in revealing many new facts and stunning surprises—and
at the same time, the little spacecraft uncovered many new mysteries.
Both before and since the *Mariner 10* mission, ground-based observations have also expanded our understanding of this intriguing planet.
At the same time, they have also added to its puzzling mysteries.

Many of the mysteries are fundamental. The closeness of Mercury's
orbit to the Sun, its amazingly high density, and its magnetic field all
raise questions about this tiny planet's origins and its history. One
whole side of Mercury remains unseen and unexplored. No mapping
mission has ever charted Mercury's features in detail. The *Mariner 10*
images did offer stunning sights of this craggy, cratered little planet.

Since then, low-resolution radar images have also shown some views of the side *Mariner 10* did not visit. Yet none of these images provides the kind of detail that scientists have gained from the high-resolution radar mapping images available for Venus. These images do not come close to the high-resolution images that have streamed earthward from Mars. And the moons of Jupiter have received much closer, longer scrutiny from the spacecraft *Galileo*.

Sending a MESSENGER

So planetologists are excited by a new mission to Mercury that NASA has been planning—a spacecraft mission called MESSENGER (for *me*rcury *s*urface, *s*pace *en*vironment, *ge*ochemistry, and *r*anging). Currently, NASA plans to launch *MESSENGER* in 2004, to arrive at Mercury in 2009. After flying by twice to get the lay of the land, the spacecraft will orbit the tiny planet for a year.

The challenges faced by this low-cost mission will be huge. The plan calls for a year-long orbiting and mapping period just 36 million miles (58 million km) from the Sun. That means the spacecraft must withstand blistering heat. The Sun shines eleven times brighter on Mercury than on Earth, and the spacecraft will skim quickly over the planet's hottest regions to keep *MESSENGER* from getting too hot from the heat reflected and radiated from the planet. Even the *Hubble Space Telescope* does not turn its sensitive eye toward Mercury for fear of frying its sensitive delicate instruments.

Getting in sync with Mercury's fast-paced orbit will take some maneuvering, too. *MESSENGER* will make two flybys past Venus for gravity assists and two flybys past Mercury to fine-tune its movements and move into orbit.

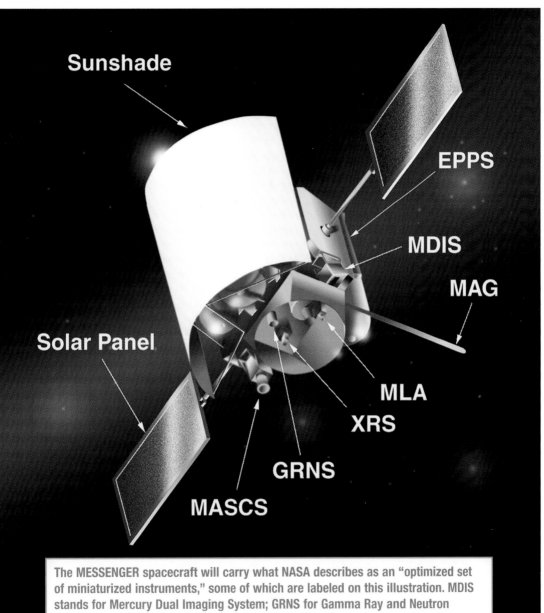

Sunshade

EPPS

MDIS

MAG

Solar Panel

MLA
XRS

GRNS

MASCS

The MESSENGER spacecraft will carry what NASA describes as an "optimized set of miniaturized instruments," some of which are labeled on this illustration. MDIS stands for Mercury Dual Imaging System; GRNS for Gamma Ray and Neutron Spectrometer; XRS for X-Ray Spectrometer; MAG for Magnetometer; MLA for Mercury Laser Altimeter; MASCS for Mercury Atmospheric and Surface Composition Spectrometer; and EPPS for Energetic Particle and Plasma Spectrometer.

MESSENGER's goals include answering some of the big questions that scientists have about Earth's second-closest neighbor. They want to know the origin of Mercury's high density. They hope to find out about the composition (*geochemistry*) and structure of its crust. Also, scientists want to know what role—if any—volcanoes may have played in forming Mercury's surface. What is the planet's *tectonic* history (relating to formation of the crust)? Scientists would also like to find out more about the ultra-thin atmosphere, Mercury's tiny magnetosphere, and the nature of its polar caps. With a fuller understanding of the innermost terrestrial planet, many insights into the evolution of the other three terrestrial planets are almost certain to be gained as well.

Mercury's ancient surfaces provide a record of some of the earliest events in the formation of our solar system. MESSENGER will give scientists a chance to take a closer look at this history—and the results are sure to broaden our understanding of the forces and processes that have shaped the rocky planets of our solar system over the past 4.5 billion years.

Ambitious European Plans

The European Space Agency (ESA) (ESA) also has plans for a mission to Mercury. Named BepiColombo, it includes three spacecraft—two orbiters (a planetary orbiter and a magnetospheric orbiter) and an exploratory probe.

Planned to launch in 2009, the BepiColombo mission spacecraft will image and map Mercury's surface. It will also examine the planet's geochemistry, gravity field, and magnetic field. Researchers expect to gain information about the planet's rotation, as well as information that will allow them to construct models of the planet's intriguing

The *Apollo 11* lunar module, called *Eagle*, casts its shadow on the surface of the Moon. Each year, manned missions to other planets become more feasible. Perhaps one day, a spacecraft will be able to land on Mercury's surface.

interior. The spacecraft will also examine particles and waves found in space in Mercury's vicinity, as well as in the solar wind close to the Sun. Finally, it will use radio science to conduct tests related to gravitational theory.

Like NASA's MESSENGER, BepiColombo will strive to find answers to some of the mysteries left behind by *Mariner 10* and, by the time of its arrival at Mercury, by MESSENGER as well. The mission's researchers hope to find out why Mercury's density is so high and how the planet's magnetic field is generated. They hope to discover clues to Mercury's geological history and they intend to find out more about Mercury's atmosphere. For example, what is Mercury made of from the inside out? What is the composition of the crust? Was there a lot of volcanism, as Robinson and Lucey's study suggests? If so, was the volcanism calm or explosive? Did Mercury once have an ocean of molten lava like the Moon's? Did it form from materials close to the Sun, or did some of the material come from further out, as well?

Scientists also want to know if the poles are capped by water ice, or at least if it is present. And they hope to discover how the planetary magnetic field interacts with the solar wind—especially without an *ionosphere* such as Earth has. They even hope to see if they can make use of the Sun nearby to run further tests on Einstein's general theory of relativity.

With these two missions, the study of Mercury promises to be a lively area of discovery, as, one by one, old mysteries may be solved and exciting new puzzles may unfold.

Missions to Mercury

Vital Statistics			
Spacecraft	**Event**	**Month/Year**	**Sponsor**
MARINER 10	Triple flyby launched	November 1973	NASA
	Flies by Venus for gravity assist	February 1974	
	First flyby	March 1974	
	Second flyby	September 1974	
	Third flyby	March 1975	
MESSENGER	Planned launch	March 2004	NASA
	Planned launch	April 2009	
BEPICOLOMBO	Planned launch	2009 or 2010	ESA
	Planned arrival	2012 or 2013	ESA

Exploring Mercury: A Timeline

ca. 356 B.C.E.	Heraclides, a Greek astronomer, puts forth the idea that Mercury and Venus orbit the Sun, not Earth.
a.d. 1881–1889	Giovanni Schiaparelli does the first complete mapping of Mercury using a telescope.
1889	Schiaparelli announces that Mercury rotates once every 88 days—the same length of time it takes to complete an orbit around the Sun.
1934	Eugenios Antoniadi publishes a detailed map of Mercury.
1965	Radar studies show that Mercury takes 58.6 Earth days to complete one rotation, proving Schiaparelli's calculation incorrect.
1973	On November 3, *Mariner 10* is launched and heads for its first observations, at Venus.

1974	On February 5, *Mariner 10* flies by Venus on its way to Mercury.
	On March 29, *Mariner 10* flies by Mercury for the first time.
	On September 21, *Mariner 10* flies by Mercury for the second time.
1975	On March 16, *Mariner 10* flies by Mercury for the third and last time.
1991	Possible evidence of ice is discovered at the poles of Mercury.
1997	Robinson and Lucey study of *Mariner 10* images.
2004	A launch is planned for MESSENGER, a NASA mapping mission to Mercury.
2009	MESSENGER is scheduled to arrive at Mercury. ESA's BepiColombo mission to Mercury is scheduled to launch.

accretion—the process of growth by a gradual buildup

asteroid—leftover chunks of material not made part of any planet during the formation of the solar system; also, part of a planet broken off by a collision

asteroid belt—the region between Mars and Jupiter, where most asteroids orbit

astronomical unit (AU)—the mean distance of Earth from the Sun. One AU is 93 million miles (150 million km); this measurement is often used to talk about distances within the solar system.

atmosphere—a layer of gases surrounding a planet or moon

axis—an imaginary line, or pole, around which a planet turns, or rotates

composition—what something, such as a planet, is made of

core—the distinct region that is located at the center of a planet. A body that has the same composition throughout is not said to have a core.

crater—a bowl-shaped depression. One type of crater, sometimes called an impact crater, is the rimmed basin caused by the impact of a meteorite, a comet, or an asteroid.

crust—the outer surface, or layer, of a planet or moon

cuneiform—a type of writing created by the Sumerians in which wedge-shaped lines form characters that convey meaning

density—how much of a substance (mass) exists in a given volume; usually measured in grams per cubic centimeter (g/cm^3)

diameter—the distance in a straight line from the surface on one side of a planet through the center to the surface on the other side

eccentric orbit—an orbit that is not a closed, perfectly round circle. An ellipse is more eccentric than a circle because even though it is closed, it is flattened, not perfectly round.

eject—to throw upward and outward

ejecta—material thrown up and out of a crater by an impact

electromagnetic spectrum—the full range of the waves and frequencies of electromagnetic radiation. Radio waves are the longest

waves in the spectrum, followed by microwaves (including radar) and then infrared rays. Visible light is about in the middle. At the other end of the spectrum are types of radiation with such short wavelengths that they are invisible to humans. These include ultraviolet (UV) waves, X-rays, and finally gamma rays, the shortest waves of all.

electron—an elementary subatomic particle that has a negative charge and is present in the makeup of all ordinary matter

flyby—a spacecraft mission that flies by a planetary object, without landing or orbiting

frequency—when measuring sound waves or electromagnetic radiation, the number of times per second a wave varies through a complete cycle (from the top of one wave to the top of the next) when measuring sound waves or electromagnetic radiation

geocentric—"Earth-centered"; refers to the concept that all astronomical objects revolve around Earth

geochemistry—the study of the composition of and chemical changes in the solid matter of a planetary body

gravity—the force of attraction between two objects. The strength of the force depends on the masses of the objects (more massive objects have a stronger pull) and how close those objects are to each other (the closer they are, the stronger the pull).

heliocentric—"Sun-centered"; refers to the concept that the planets of our solar system revolve around the Sun

hypothesis (pl. hypotheses)—an explanation of a set of facts that can be tested; the basis for a theory

infrared (IR) radiation—a type of electromagnetic radiation that has long wavelengths, just beyond visible red light in the spectrum, and so is invisible to humans but can be recorded by special instruments

interstellar—located among or having to do with the stars

ionosphere—the portion of Earth's upper atmosphere where enough ions and electrons are present to affect radio transmission

magma—molten rock beneath a planet's surface; a slush of crystals, gases, and liquid rock *magnetosphere*—a vast region of electromagnetic radiation and electrically charged particles extending out from a planet; caused by the interaction of the planet's magnetic field and the solar wind

mantle—a geologically different region located between the crust and the core of a planetary body (a planet, moon, or asteroid)

mantle plumes—hot, upward flowing currents of magma or molten rock within the mantle

mass—the amount of material a body contains (usually measured in grams or kilograms)

meteorite—a chunk of a rock from space that has landed on the surface of a planet or moon

meteoroid—a small chunk of material not included in any planet during formation; part of a planet that has been broken off by a collision (see *asteroid*)

nuclear fusion—a process that takes place in the core of the Sun and other stars, releasing enormous energy when two atoms of hydrogen combine to form helium

nebula—a cloud of interstellar gas or dust, or both

nucleus—the central portion of an atom that is composed of protons and neutrons (subatomic particles having no charge). Hydrogen is the only element with a nucleus consisting of only one proton and no neutron.

orbit—the path traced out by an object as it revolves around another body; also, the act of traveling such a path

perihelion—the point in an orbit at which a planet is closest to the Sun

planetologist—a specialist in the study of planets (planetary bodies) and moons

precession—a wobble or variation in the orbit or spin of an astronomical body

proton—a stable subatomic particle that has a positive charge.

radar—from *ra*dio *d*etection *a*nd *r*anging; the practice of bouncing very high-frequency radio waves off the surface of an object to detect its distance, shape, position, and other characteristics

radio telescope—a type of telescope that combines a radio antenna (a large satellite dish) and receiver to gather and "listen to" radio waves emitted by celestial objects

reflecting telescope—a type of telescope that uses mirrors to gather light and relay images to the observer

refracting telescope—a type of telescope that uses lenses to gather light and magnify objects

resolution—in an image or photograph, the ability to display detail. A camera that has high resolution can capture extensive detail with a high level of accuracy.

revolution—one complete tour in an orbit around the Sun. The Earth revolves around the Sun, making a revolution in one year, while Mercury takes eighty-eight Earth days.

revolve—to move in a path, or orbit, around another object; the Earth revolves around the Sun, making a complete trip in one year; Mercury takes 88 days

rotate—to turn on its an axis. Earth rotates once in twenty-four hours; Mercury takes fifty-nine Earth days.

rotation—one complete turn on a planet's axis

sinkhole—a depression in a land area that is connected to a limestone cave or cavern, often caused by the collapse of a cavern roof

solar nebula—a primitive cloud of gas and dust from which the Sun and the planets were born

solar wind—a stream of highly charged particles that flows at high speeds from the Sun's surface

tectonic—relating to the deformation of a planet's crust

terrestrial planets—Earth and the planets of the solar system that most closely resemble it; specifically Earth, Mercury, Mars, and Jupiter

thrust faults—a fault, or crack in a planet's crust, in which the upper side appears to have been pushed upward

topography—the description or mapping of a planet's physical surface features

ultraviolet (UV) rays—"black light"; the type of radiation with wavelengths just shorter than violet light. UV rays are invisible to humans.

To Find Out More

The news from space changes fast, so it's always a good idea to check the copyright date on books, CD-ROMs, and videotapes to make sure that you are getting up-to-date information. One good place to look for current information from NASA is U.S. government depository libraries. There are several in each state.

Books

Brimner, Larry Dane. *Mercury.* New York: Children's Press, 1998.

Campbell, Ann Jeanette. *The New York Public Library Amazing Space: A Book of Answers for Kids.* New York: John Wiley & Sons, 1997.

Daily, Robert. *Mercury.* (First Books: The Solar System Series). New York: Franklin Watts, 1996.

Dickinson, Terence. *Other Worlds: A Beginner's Guide to Planets and Moons.* Willowdale, Ontario: Firefly Books, 1995.

Gustafson, John. *Planets, Moons and Meteors.* (The Young Stargazer's Guide to the Galaxy) series. New York: Julian Messner, 1992.

Hartmann, William K., and Don Miller. *The Grand Tour.* New York: Workman Publishing, 1993.

Simon, Seymour. *Mercury.* New York: William Morrow & Co., 1998.

Strom, Robert G. *Mercury: The Elusive Planet.* Washington, D.C.: Smithsonian Institution Press, 1987.

Vogt, Gregory L. *Mercury.* Brookfield, CT.: Millbrook Press, 1998.

————. *The Solar System Facts and Exploration.* Scientific American Sourcebooks series. New York: Twenty-First Century Books, 1995.

CD-ROM

Beyond Planet Earth, for Macintosh and PC (DOS, Windows, OS2)
Discovery Channel School Multimedia
P.O. Box 970
Oxon Hill, MD 20750-0970
Phone: 888-892-3494
Fax: 301-567-9553
This interactive journey to the planets, including Mercury, comprises video from NASA and Voyager missions to other planets and more than 200 two hundred photographs.

Video Ttapes

Discover Magazine: Solar System
Available from:
Discovery Channel School
P.O. Box 970

Oxon Hill, MD   20750-0970
Phone: 888-892-3494;
Fax: 301-567-9553

Organizations and Online Sites

Several of the online websites listed below here are NASA sites, with
links to many other interesting sources of information about Mercury and the other planets of the solar system. You can also sign up
to receive NASA news on many subjects via e-mail.

Astronomical Society of the Pacific

http://astrosociety.org
390 Ashton Avenue
San Francisco, CA   94112

The Astronomy Café

http://theastronomycafe.net
Astronomer and NASA scientist Sten Odenwald answers questions
and offers news and articles relating to astronomy and space.

NASA Ask a Space Scientist

http://image.gsfc.nasa.gov/poetry/ask/askmag.html#list
At this interactive page, NASA scientists answer questions about
astronomy, space, and space missions. This site also offers archives
and fact sheets.

NASA Newsroom
http://www.nasa.gov/newsinfo/newsroom.html
This site contains NASA's latest press releases, status reports, and fact sheets and includes a NASA News Archive for past reports and a search button for the NASA Web. You can sign up for e-mail versions of all NASA press releases.

The Nine Planets: A Multimedia Tour of the Solar System
http://www.seds.org/nineplanets/nineplanets/nineplanets.html
The Students for the Exploration and Development of Space at the University of Arizona have compiled excellent material on Mercury and other planets.

Planetary Missions
http://nssdc.gsfc.nasa.gov/planetary/projects.html
This one-stop shopping center to a wealth of information has links to all current and past NASA missions.

The Planetary Society
http://www.planetary.org/
65 North Catalina Avenue
Pasadena, CA   91106-2301

Sky Online

http://www.skyandtelescope.com

This website for *Sky and Telescope* magazine and other publications of Sky Publishing Corporation has a good weekly news section on general space and astronomy news. The site also contains many good tips for amateur astronomers, as well as a nice selection of links. A list of science museums, planetariums, and astronomy clubs organized by state helps locate nearby places to visit.

Space.com

http://www.space.com

This site covers the latest news in space and astronomy, including missions and launches, science and astronomy, space-related technology, and SETI (the search for extraterrestrial intelligence), and the search for life on other planets.

Welcome to the Planets

http://pds.jpl.nasa.gov/planets/

Created by the California Institute of Technology for NASA's Jet Propulsion Laboratory, this site offers a tour of the solar system, with lots of pictures and information.

Windows to the Universe
http://www.windows.ucar.edu/tour/link=/windows3.html
This NASA site, developed by the University of Michigan, includes
sections on "Our Planet," "Our Solar System," "Space Missions,"
and "Kids' Space." You can choose from presentation levels of beginner, intermediate, or advanced.

Places to Visit

Places to Visit
Check the Internet (*www.http: //skyandtelescope.com* is a good place to
start), your local visitor's center, or your phone directory for planetariums, science museums, and other places of interest near you. Here
are several suggestions. Some of these places are so big that it takes
days to see everything. Others are smaller but still well worth an
afternoon of your time. Some are famous; others are not. Each is
worth a visit.

Ames Research Center
Moffett Field, CA 94035
http://www.arc.nasa.gov/
Located near Mountain View and Sunnyvale on the San Francisco
Peninsula, Ames Research Center welcomes visitors. This NASA
branch heads the search for extraterrestrial life. Drop-in visitors are
welcome and admission is free.

Center of Science and Technology
333 West Broadway Street
Columbus, OH 43215
www.cosi.org/
A very interesting museum with many creative exhibits. After you've seen some of the exhibits take a ride on the high-wire unicycle!

Discovery Place
301 North Tryon Street
Charlotte, NC 28202
www.discoveryplace.org/
Wide ranging and creative exhibits.

Exploratorium
3601 Lyon Street
San Francisco, CA 94123
http://www.exploratorium.edu/
Here you'll find internationally acclaimed interactive science exhibits, including astronomy subjects.

Houston Museum of Natural Science
1 Hermann Loop Drive
Houston, TX 77030
www.hmns.org/

They also have an astronomical observatory that features one of the largest of all telescopes that's open to public viewing. The George Observatory is located in Brazos Bend State Park. There are regularly scheduled times for public viewing.

The Montshire Museum
1 Montshire Road
Norwich, VT 05055
www.montshire.net/
This is a small, creative, high-quality, hands-on science museum.

The Museum of Science
Science Park
Boston, MA 02114
www.mos.org/
This museum takes days to explore and those are days well spent.

The National Museum of Science and Technology
1867 St. Laurent Blvd.
Ottawa, Ontario K1G 5A3
Canada.
www.science-tech.nmstc.ca/
This museum is huge. It contains many exhibits and they're all well-done.

The National Air and Space Museum
Washington, D.C. 20560-0321
www.nasm.si.edu
This is part of the Smithsonian Institution and it's one of the great museums of its kind in the world. Take time to see the permanent exhibit entitled Looking@Earth.

Odyssium
11211-142 Street
Edmonton, Alberta T5M 4A1
Canada
www.odyssium.com/
This museum has undergone a lot of changes over the years. It keeps getting better.

Your Local Astronomy Club
http://skyandtelescope.com/
Join your local astronomy club and see Mercury for yourself. Most astronomy clubs have monthly meetings where you can learn all sorts of things, and they'll occasionally set up their telescopes for public viewing. Most serious amateur astronomers have already seen Mercury through their own telescopes. Mercury isn't hard to see if you know where to look, but you can't see it without a telescope. Call ahead of a regularly scheduled public viewing. Explain that you have

a special interest in Mercury. If Mercury is visible the night of the viewing, I'll bet one of the club members will be happy to show it to you. To find an astronomy club in your area consult your local library or local science museum or consult the directory maintained by the magazine, *Sky and Telescope*, at the webaddress given above.

Index

Bold numbers indicate illustrations

Ray Spangenburg and **Kit Moser** write together about science and technology. This husband-and-wife writing team has written nearly fifty books and one hundred articles, including a five-book series on the history of science and a series on space exploration and astronomy. Their writing has taken them on some great adventures. They have flown on NASA's Kuiper Airborne Observatory (a big plane carrying a telescope). They have also visited the Deep Space Network in the Mojave Desert, where signals from spacecraft are collected. They have even flown in zero gravity on an experimental NASA flight. Ray and Kit live and write in Carmichael, California, with their Boston Terrier, F. Scott Fitz.

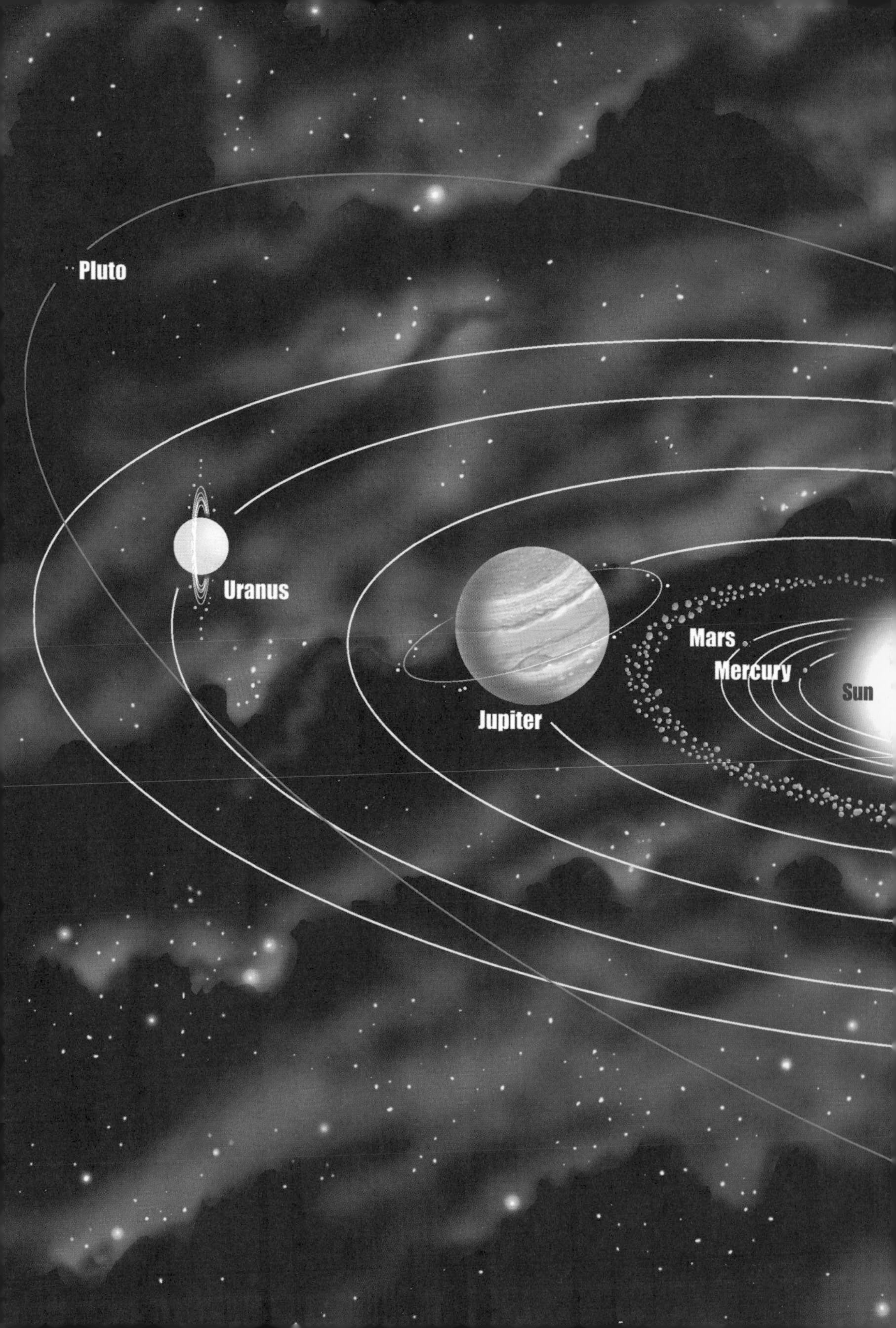
Pluto
Uranus
Jupiter
Mars
Mercury
Sun